Dark Discourse with the Sleepy Cat

A Caregiver's World of Life and Death at 3 AM

John Nelson

PREFACE – 2018

Several years ago a client asked me, "If I ever have to die intentionally, will you help me?" We may have been talking at the time about Washington State's recent Death With Dignity law; but the question could just as well have come out of the blue – with Ginny, context was superfluous. I said something like "Yeah, sure, whatever", and we went on with our planned computer work.

I received an unexpected call from Ginny last spring: she was suddenly experiencing severe and worrisome neurological symptoms, which seemed to be getting worse, and she could not get any help from her doctor. Ginny's reasoning and communicating abilities were already impaired, and she didn't know what to do next.

My partner and I immediately took on the task of patient advocacy for Ginny. During the next weeks we found new doctors for her, scheduled office visits and tests, and took her to appointments. But we quickly added the resources of hospice and the "End of Life Washington" volunteer group when we all discovered Ginny had untreatable advanced brain tumors. She was expected to lose mental competence within weeks. Ginny decided to die before that could happen – intentionally, sanely, and surrounded by her loving family and friends.

During Ginny's last month, her new doctors were all in the downtown Seattle Swedish Medical complex. For those appointments I was parking in the Swedish garages, dropping Ginny off at the Swedish front doors, walking their hallways and sky bridges from building to building, sitting in lobbies and waiting rooms, all as if for the first time.

But one day, while I was simply walking down a hallway, complete and total recall dropped onto me: this was exactly where Lynn and I had together spent much of the last several years of Lynn's life. The whole place was all suddenly as familiar to me as my living room. And there was more: Lynn's esteemed oncologist, from all those years ago, had now been randomly chosen to be Ginny's new oncologist. I was shaken. During his intake exam with Ginny, he talked with her a while; then he stopped, looked at me a moment, and said "I think I know you…?" (Yes, indeed you do.)

Ginny died within weeks, and my job as her advocate was done. But the events of that month reawakened in me the memory of my previous life.

My beloved partner Lynn died exactly eleven years before Ginny's death. This story – written during the last of my time with Lynn, written to save myself, written in the middle of sleepless nights, often in desperation, written because it was all I could do – sat untouched and unread for those eleven years. Ginny's death resurrected Lynn's death for me, and resurrected this story.

This is not Lynn's story. As overwhelming and excruciating as her fatal illness was to her, I understand that it was but a small part of the total magnificence of her life, and that life goes on.

No, this isn't much about Lynn: that woman who died of cancer has her own story.

This is the story of the caregiver.

DARK DISCOURSE – 2001-2007

The Sleepy Cat

Middle of the night breakfast cereal.
Beside me, deep yellow eyes appear, still sleepy.
Find the feather. Lick the bowl. Squirm. Roll. Do cute.
Wet, warm tongue, on her own furry arm, then on mine.

Yellow eyes look up at blue ones:

Time stops.

Presence.
Pure love.
Contentment.

Maybe everything's going to be Ok.

Two Worlds

Pop Awake Now!
   …sleeping, dreaming; continue…
No! Awake!
  pee, return.
   …my college class, some girl, terrible mistake, embarrassed, laughed at…
Awake!
  ok. hunger? no, panic. something wrong? house? Lynn!?
  soft snoring: good. find earplugs, roll over, close eyes.
   …huge menacing ship full of grotesque aliens, jumping to translight-speed, deadly bomb delivered; Lynn's neck, horribly misshapen, blossoming with red lumpy tumors squeezing nerve and tendon, ready to break open…
Awake!!
  ok; go downstairs. cat (always), her spot on the couch. quiet, dark, warm. eat yogurt. stare at the fire. relax.

Downstairs, even in the middle of the night, life is what I've always known, predictable.
Upstairs, beside Lynn, there's evil lurking, creeping, seeking further silent penetration.
Can't I just stay downstairs? Can't she just come with me?

"Bob"

Bob phones for Lynn. Not all the time, but more frequently now.

She talks to him. I don't think she always wants to, because sometimes it's days before she returns his messages.

Then they talk quietly and intently, and I get a sense there's something secret going on that I can't be part of it. It's almost as if they're planning something.

I don't like it. Sure, I don't know anything about the guy, but even his name bugs me. Bob, he says. Bob. He sounds too slick to me, like a salesman. Bob, from Forest Lawn Memorial.

It's just a gut feeling, but I'm really scared that someday he'll take her away from me.

My priorities:

(1) Keep it together. Survive. Keep myself functional; get Lynn what she needs; keep us fed and comfortable.

(2) Sit beside Lynn. Touch her. Be with her.

(3) Keep my business going, take care of my clients. Take care of myself. Learn and grow if I can. Try to stay happy.

Days and Nights, Months and Years

1:30 am. December. Uncontrollable shaking, or was it irregular heartbeat? Probably both. Emergency room. Too busy, lights too bright. Wide awake.

 Daytime.

11:45 pm. October. I got up at noon, Lynn at 4:00 pm. Got dressed, then some napping. Food. Napping. Now, we're finally starting with today's Star Treks.

 Daytime.

1:30 pm. July. Typical day in the hospital treatment center waiting room. *Waiting* room. Exhausted, both of us. Her head on my lap, my head in my hands. Even solitaire is way too much work.

 Nighttime.

3:50 am. August. Thinking, worrying, hungry and wide awake. Eat some, write some, play with the cat. It's become routine. Middle of the night writing feels like my day job now.

 My daytime.

4:00 am. June. Hospital room easy chair. Oncology floor visitor room sofa. Visitor room chair. Hospital room chair. Lynn's tiny bed. Visitor room sofa. No good; just get up.

 Isn't it daytime yet?

8:00 am. January. Get up, shower, dress. Wake Lynn, get ready for scans. Talk to Lynn. Rub feet, hold hand. Wake Lynn. Help her sit up. Wake Lynn. Help her stand, walk to bathroom, get in shower, sit down, turn on water, hot. Go downstairs, make coffee, feed cat, eat something myself. Go back upstairs: shower still on. Wake Lynn! (What interesting red marks.)

Middle of the damn night.

3:45 am. May. She made a noise. It was nothing, but I had to get up and go check. Back to the sofa. Toss and turn. Entertain the cat. Think of things that have gone wrong. Think of things that could still go wrong. Will go wrong. Listen for her breath. Wait for the next one. Hope.

Feels like nightfall.

She's Dying

Use the goddamn right lane! Don't slow down on the ramp! Idiot! You pull in at about 30 and slam straight over in a panic into the second lane, brakes on and blinker wailing. Then you fucking slow down and cut across all three lanes to make your exit. Did you forget where your damn exit was? Or did that phone in your ear make you too stupid to see where you are! What's your goddamn problem!? Gimme a break and get the fuck off the road! And that new intersection on 220th: what the hell were they thinking? I can tell you twenty ways the old one was better! If they don't have a dozen accidents a week, it's a miracle! Goddamn left turns hold up the whole road! And if you're not lucky, you drive right into oncoming traffic. Those idiots! You'd think they wanted us all to die...

Oh God. No. No.

Problems

Abdominal swelling
Amnesia
Amputation
Anger
Avoidance behavior
Baldness
Bleeding
Bone pain
Bony lumps
Broken hip
Changed hair color and texture
Cognition problems
Colds
Collapsed veins
Compromised immune system
Confusion
Constipation
Coughing
Cracked ribs
Decreased clotting
Dehydration
Depression
Diarrhea
Difficulty swallowing
Difficulty handling eating utensils
Difficulty reading and writing
Digestion problems
Disorientation
Double vision
Dry eyes
Dry lips
Dry mouth
Dry skin
Ear pain
Elevated blood pressure
Enlarged liver
Extreme fatigue
Fainting
Falls
Fast heart rate
Fear
Feeling of helplessness
Fine motor control loss
Flexibility loss
Food sensitivities
Fractured vertebrae
Halitosis
Hallucinations
Headaches
Heart damage
Hip motion limitations
Hot flashes
Incontinence
Infection

Irrational thoughts
Irregular breathing
Irregular heartbeat
Isolation
Jaundice
Lifting restrictions
Loss of ability to use TV remote
Loss of employment
Loss of friends
Low blood pressure
Low red cell count
Lymphedema
Mouth sores
Nausea
Neck tumors
No appetite
Painful breathing
Painful intercourse
Painful urination
Painful walking
Panic
Radiation burns
Rasping breath
Risk of blood clot
Risk of stroke
Sadness
Scars
Sexual disfunction
Skin eruptions
Slurred speech
Sore throat
Swollen leg and foot
Taste and smell changes
Teeth problems
Tremors
Trouble catching breath
Vaginal dryness
Vertigo
Vision changes
Weakness
Weeping
Weight gain
Weight loss
Death

Treatments

Amitriptyline 10mg
Amoxicillin 500mg
Anzemet 100mg
Arimidex 1mg
Atropine 1%
Cephalexin Keflex 250mg
Cephalexin Keflex 500mg
Citalopram 40mg
Clonazepam 0.5mg
Cyclobenzaprine 10mg
Cyproheptadine 4mg
Dexamethasone 2mg
Dexamethasone 4mg
Effexor 37.5mg
Effexor 75mg
Effexor 150mg
Erythromycin opth
Fentanyl 50mcg/hr 72hr
Haloperidol (Haldol) 0.5mg
Hydromorphone (Dilaudid) 2mg
Kytril Granisetron HCl 1mg
Levaquin 500mg
Lexapro Escitalopram 10mg
Lorazepam 0.5mg
Lorazepam 1mg
Lorazepam 5mg
Meclizine 12.5mg

Methylin 5mg
Metoclopramide (Reglan) 10mg
Morphone Sulfate 20mg
Naproxen 550mg
Oxycodone 5mg
Oxycodone 20mg
Prochlorperazine 10mg
Prochlorperazine 25mg
Prozac 20mg
Sulfamethoxazole 8mg
Tamoxifen 20mg
Trazodone 50mg
Warfarin 2mg
Xeloda Capecitabine 500mg
Zofran 8mg
Zyrtec 10mg
Hydrocodone 500mg

Solutions

Multiple Choice

(A) Here's what's wrong. Here's how my life SUCKS. Here's where I'm screwing up. Here's how I feel about it. Here's where people are screwing me up. Here's EXACTLY what they need to do to fix it!

(B) Nothing's wrong. Wasn't the news interesting today. Wasn't church interesting last Sunday. Wasn't that book interesting. Isn't the weather interesting. Yeah, Lynn's doing Ok. I'm Ok I guess.

(C) …nothing…

no story   no plan   no memory   no expectation   no need   no habit   no knowledge

                                        see something: what? what?

    touch someone: yes! (or) no!
     smell, taste: aaahh!

                    oh, music!   oh!

  write: here, now. gone, now.

    speak.

                                 …nothing…

Today

Good news! Today cancer is irrelevant!
Today I have three clients and I send a photo proof off to the printers.
Today I get to talk with some old friends.
Today I write and feel and think and decide and change.
Today my life continues unimpeded.

<u>Mister</u> **Death**

Sometime yesterday, when I wasn't paying attention, death took a shower. Shaved, got a haircut. Bought some new clothes, something besides black. Lost the scythe.

Unexpectedly, death isn't so fearsome. It's just death. True, I'm talking about her death, not mine, and I can't even guess what this is like for her. But for me, the real bad stuff is already done, or at least stared down. Now, it's down to the dying itself. There's the physical part, the process, the bodily changes. Truth be told, that's kind of fascinating. Horrible, and fascinating. And somewhat predictable.

And there's the spiritual part. Passing. Transition. Dropping the body. That's a real mystery, and not a tragedy. Again, it's not me doing the dying. But I believe if I stay quiet and alert, I might learn something important. Might find a way to let death be part of life – my life.

Now that it's becoming more than simply a disreputable cartoon character, I might even be willing to keep company with the new Mister Death for a while.

Emptyfulness

I have nothing. I am nothing.
Only need.
Only pain.
Only loss.
Only deprivation.
Only emptiness.

I have nothing to bring you.
Only my empty self, full of nothing.

My self.
Present.
Here, now.
With you.

Enough?

Scarves Somewhere
(Conversation with Lynn's sister)

Thirteen amazing knit scarves. See, the picture here shows how beautiful they are, arranged on display like that! Colors you couldn't imagine together! And soft...

They started out as a teaching project for the cancer support knitting group, and she got a little carried away. I don't know if you can even get yarn like that anymore. She sold a couple, for less than the cost of the yarn; but they were donated to a fundraiser, so she didn't care.

You should let your daughter look through the rest, choose one to remember her aunt by – now, soon, while Lynn is still able to give it to her and tell her the story herself.

Now, where did we put those scarves? Oh, well, I'll find them someday...

The Shape of Lynn

I live in a tangled and raveled mountain of Lynn's possessions. Earring, skirt, vase, lotion, shoe, bread pan, treadmill, pencil, bass, mascara, scrub brush, photo, sofa, book, hair gel, printer, rug, receipt, wall hanging, choker, sock, piano, phone, car, cat box, paint can, puppet, coat, CD, pill bottle, yarn, glass bowl, video game, chocolate bar, scissors, refrigerator, walker, extension cord, blanket, lamp, window, and on and on.

In the center of the mountain, invisibly maintaining it all, is the will of Lynn. All is hers, chosen and gathered and held tight by her existence and desire.

For now, this world of Lynn is the world I take for granted and never really notice. Tomorrow, or next week, or next month, Lynn will die. The will at the center of the mountain will suddenly collapse, leaving an empty hole in my world the shape of Lynn.

Houses

I dreamed one night of two houses.

(One)

The house was burning!
Not mine, but I was living there, attending to the house.
The owner, a woman, was fighting beside me.
We were both committed, but exhausted; this was not a new struggle. In fact the house had been burning for a long time. There were no flames. Rather, there were long glowing tongues of bright crimson here and there throughout the house, just under the surface – waving and pulsing like northern lights, or snakes, threatening to finally burst into flame. These were our enemy.

I was anxiously playing a cooling stream of water on one dangerous hot spot outside the bedroom. The woman was trying to soothe another just inside. I voiced the growing conviction that had been whirling silently between us: We've got to do something different! This is our last chance. There might be more experts we could call, resources we could still find.
The angry crimson near her exploded, and she could only say, "I don't think we have time..."

In panic, I thought, well, let's save at least something – and I saw all the books...

I awoke at that point, and I squelched the urge to race around unplugging appliances and extinguishing pilot lights. No, the fire that horrified me was real, but the house it would soon devour was softly asleep beside me.

(Two)

My house was nearly empty, just a few pieces of furniture and a couple of rugs. But it was an intriguing rambling house, with quirky and elegant details. I wandered some, and started meeting people, workers in the house. One team was fixing a little hidden roof, and I watched a bit and talked. Some were repairing an electrical system, and I helped them solve a puzzling problem. I was surprised and grateful: even though I couldn't be there to care for the house, it was in good hands.

In the days after these dreams, I thought a lot about "the books". They seemed to be the substance of Lynn's life: her skills, passions, talents, secrets, dreams – all seemingly moments away from being lost forever.

But a friend later showed me a different interpretation of the books in my dream. They are the wisdom from the journey. And it is not lost. Within the dream, I thought of the books within space and time, and I valued them above anything else, believing I had to act if they were to be saved. Now, awake, I know that the wisdom from this journey – not facts, or even individual personal memories, but imperishable and inexpressible understanding of higher truths

learned together in our shared experience – this wisdom is the goal
and the sure prize of what currently appears as calamity.

(Revise)

Still, the house burns. The first dream ended, incomplete, in panic,
as there is ongoing panic in our lives. But I cannot let that be the
final word. I can finish that dream, even now, as I wish, and so
choose how I shape and understand this waking nightmare as well:

..."I don't think we have time." And, yes, there was suddenly fire
erupting everywhere in the house! But it was ugly red and vicious
only for a moment – then everything turned pure white. The glowing tongues and the erupting flames were no longer consuming the
house; they *were* the house, the real house – now ever brighter,
quicker, dancing, exploding upwards and outwards, faster and higher
than seemed possible. We were illuminated and transformed in the
brilliant white phosphorescence. And the house – or what it became
– endured. As I witnessed the process, standing beside Lynn, I saw
there was no loss. No panic, now, no fight. Just grace.

"A New Heaven and a New Earth"

My hand is on her, as always:
her leg, the small of her back, her heart.
She can create no response. (Why am I here?)
Finally – after some time – she nestles a finger or two into my hand.
All else is forgotten!

Thank you, for giving...

We two live out a deep and binding pact.

Our union is for giving and receiving,
though giving and receiving seem at odds.
Must that received be always given first?
Unwillingly received, is it a gift?
Unwilling gift, still gift? What benefit?
When gift is death, receiving feels like death!

What awesome need invoked such dire contract?

We love each other still, but not the same
as when we first loved: hotly, thoughtlessly,
from desperate need to mate, body and soul!
We lost that heat, replaced it soon with ice;
and illness makes it worse. Promises
of reconciliation fade away,
along with energy, hair, appetite.
(Was last night just another night, when I
– or she – rolled over, faced away, feigned sleep,
refused request for touch? Or was it our
last chance, in this lifetime, to make love...?)

Exactly how is it a gift, when love
is not returned? Expectations not
fulfilled? Desires not met? Needs ignored?
What gift, exactly, tells a partner: No,

this one thing that you need, I forbid!
Not now from me, nor any other, will you get
the warmth that feeds your life and heals your heart.

Exactly how is it a gift, to spend
these cold years with impending death, devote
our time to pain, dote on loss, attend
so carefully each ugly new attack?

The mind can know no more.

The heart moves on...

The gift - forgiveness - is not anything
that can be known by these two selves, not while
their histories and stories bound their lives,
or difference of opinion or belief
creates illusion of two separate souls, and they
believe the fraud.

I float above these lives, and see a glimpse
of repetitions: generations past,
each learning from the last to teach the next
to hurt, ignore, neglect, abuse, cause pain...

(And so we claim, each, our inheritance –

hers, power used in place of love; and mine,
the lessons of unworthiness and guilt –
which intermesh so perfectly it seems
as if by plan, as if to give a gift…)

From high above these lives, I understand
that giver and receiver of this gift
conspire, each taking on the role of both,
until it blurs who's who.

Above these lives (where harm is given and
received), are higher lives: there is forgiveness planned.
There, we're the same, there is no "you" and "me".
In deep love, there, we plan together lives
like ours.

> Lynn (highest Lynn), we give you deep gratitude,
> (forgiving you) for giving us this journey.
> John (highest John), we give you deep gratitude,
> (forgiving you) for giving us this journey.

Don't sleep!

Your eyes roll back, your lids often don't quite close. Your brow creases. The corners of your lips turn down, looking so sad, so old. Your jaw sags, or your mouth moves as if you are calling for help, or trying to tell me something. You look too thin, your bald head too fragile. Your face is not the face of Lynn; it's what I've seen in paintings, in movies, and once, on my father: the face of all dead. Lynn is gone.

Then you awaken. Now I know you! Your face is your own again. You smile. Your eyes see me. You're funny, and you laugh at the cat.

Sometime soon, you will not awaken.

Please, don't sleep!

Has the Time Come!??

Oh! Has the time come? so soon? But I'm not ready! She's not ready – is she? There's so much to be done! Things we still have to talk about: love, forgiveness, mistakes, misunderstandings, untold gratitude. So many questions and mysteries to be solved, important things I've never told her, she's never told me. She hasn't planned her funeral, how can she leave? And what about her family? They don't know, they haven't prepared. I don't know if they could. What if she dies tonight – right now! Her breathing is so slow and uneven. Kathy hasn't even heard yet, and she's not coming over till tomorrow. What would she think, if I let Lynn die too soon! There are still bills to be paid. Can I sign Lynn's name after she's dead? Pay online? We should pay bills now, quickly! I can't get stuck with those, if she's gone. Wait, the estate covers that; where's her sister? That's her job. We have to call her! Should I call them? Can she call them? Does she want to? Does she want people around? Friends visiting? Do I have their names and numbers? Which ones? What would they do? What does she want?

Maybe not. Maybe it's just a passing problem, and another round of chemo will put her back right. She's been this much out of it before, though never on such a small amount of pain meds.

Oh, no! The doctor says no more chemo! So this is really the beginning of the end!? He said, we can't get you better than you are now. But the steroid: that can cause some of this. We'll quit that. Maybe she'll come back, be herself again!?
No, it's not the steroid, it's liver damage. That's terrible! No way to fix that! This is it!

The Glowing One

Lynn,

the Lynn who stands white-clad, tall and bright, glowing,
in the place where the other "I" meet her, myself white-clad and glowing:

I greet you in the way we cannot speak: God, as God. Namaste.

I am so happy, so happy to see you!
I have missed you, already, though I met you here just yesterday!
I have always missed you, and only discovered you, the glowing one,
here in this no-place, so recently!

Do we cry together, looking at our bodies, there – both dying, both living?
Do we love them (us), and bathe them in deepest, richest, softest and most holy compassion?
Do they notice, and cry together, with us?
(Yes, yes, we do.)

Do we do as they have asked, pour Love and Grace and Peace into their lives?
Do they feel lifted and held in tender arms, do they sigh and relax?
Do they know our unknowable Love for them?
(Yes, Oh yes, we do!)

(My heart breaks at the depth of this pain, and the height of this Love!
And I say, break me, break me, empty me, leave me wailing and sobbing
from despair and bliss together!)

Oh, John, my sweet, my love! Lynn, my precious, my darling!
I hold you, I forgive you, I bless you, I thank you!
We are whole, now, now, now! Ever now!

Place and no-place joined: all that is, is now.

Gently return, now, my darlings:
there is more weeping for you yet, more fear, more pain.
And it will never touch you, for you are empty.
You are the glowing one. You are God.

Bowl of Noodles

These are the same noodles, aren't they?

Two days ago, gazing into a bowl of noodles gave me an image of Lynn forever alive, beyond death, pouring out pure love and joy.

Today, the bowl of noodles shows me most clearly and painfully the loss, the day by day, hour by hour, moment by moment unbearable loss of the Lynn I love.

Are these different noodles? Or have they gone bad?

No, today they just have tears in them.

The Friday Lynn

If only we could go for a little walk, like we used to.

If only she could eat a good meal, like she did just yesterday!

If only she could talk about something besides her hallucinations; it wasn't this bad yesterday!

If only she could drink something – she was drinking a little yesterday.

If only she could get out of bed again!

If only she could just sit up.

If only she could whisper some words, like yesterday!

If only she would open her eyes and really see me, like she did yesterday.

If only she could just squeeze my hand!

If only she were still breathing.

If only she were still warm.

If only she were still here.

Moment of Panic

Where's the safe deposit box key!??

Oh, yeah – just where we should have guessed: in a coat pocket, right there with the wads of money, used tissues, and packet of Oreos.

Even dead, Lynn is still Lynn.

The Hidden Red Pouch

A large piece of amber. Didn't I buy that for her in Bali? Or did she buy it for herself?

A pair of old blue cut glass earrings. Her maternal grandmother's, we think.

Her other grandmother's ring, often mentioned, very precious. A single remnant of that life, now preserved only as a name (which I can't quite remember).

Another ring, the one she designed for her own wedding: the only thing, apparently, worth keeping from that relationship.

A newer ring, Black Hills Gold. Beautiful, valuable, but never worn; why?

A small tarnished gold chain, well-used. Obviously important to her, but I don't know why. I'll just ask her… No, wait; that would have been yesterday.

How to talk to people who are alive

How can they not see there's a big piece of me missing? My arm is torn out. I walk with a horrible limp. The side of my face is raw and bleeding.

How can they talk about the traffic conditions coming in from the airport, or their daughter's children's soccer games, or tomorrow's napkin folding pattern? Won't they glance up and gasp, seeing me transparent and ghastly from walking with the dead?

I have to talk to them simply, like they're disadvantaged children. Like drunks, I have to ignore most of what they're saying. In my altered state, I have to speak as if to tourists from Wichita who have bumbled in to my vision quest, unaware of the luminous streaks of significance flying off from every word, every motion. Unaware of the din of echoes from every moment in the last two weeks, surrounding me like a chorus. Unaware that time stopped at that instant, and is now going backwards as well as forwards, and the before and the after mix and froth in eddies and whirlpools, and I cannot tell where I am, or who.

Fortunately, my vision quest leaves me both dead and alive, and so able to accomplish the impossible: bring heart to heartlessness. I can grasp the rote recitation of trip to mall, and with one twist, deftly transform it into dreamy visits to arctic circle and equator.

Effortlessly nudge the cost of print cartridges into the fragility of the Great Barrier Reef. Shatter an endless loop of complaints with a single movement. Break an offensive tradition with a yawn.

I can, since time is going backwards as well as forwards, place my hands on a frozen chest and watch it take its first breath. I can touch a cold heart and feel it become warm. I can place my fingers on dark eyes and watch them open and perceive me, perhaps for the first time. I can listen as confusion sorts itself out into clarity and purpose.

Do I ask for healing for myself? When they speak, they probably believe they are comforting me.
They cannot. For now, I listen only to the dead.

Death, and...

My life goes on.

I really wasn't ready for that.

How could I have known that ordinary, day to day events would resume?
How could I care about telephone bills and special offers?
Or global warming?
Or eating, or brushing my teeth?

Sometimes it seems disloyal to continue living, when she's not.
Sometimes just anticlimactic.
How could anything I do now compare with what she did? what we did?

As much as I wanted to be done with the endless responsibility for
endless pain – I never believed it would end without me.

Memories Now Become Nightmares

• Lynn isn't conscious; a nurse is here. I roll Lynn too far and too quickly while helping the nurse change her: Lynn moans, her unseeing eyes fly open in panic of falling, and her arms flail helplessly for support. (I feel ashamed for ignorant and inconsiderate things I did when Lynn wasn't able to tell me what she needed.)

• Lynn is asking me about the "bad medicine". She knows I'd thought dexamethazone was the cause of her confusion, and she asks if she's still on the bad medicine. I have to tell her that it isn't the dex after all, it's her liver, and the doctor said this isn't going to get better. (That conversation was – still is – really heartbreaking, especially since even asking me the question was right at the edge of Lynn's ability by that time.)

• I'm away from the house a full day, leaving Lynn with an incompetent and thoughtless hired caregiver. Lynn is confused and barely able to walk even with assistance, but she's making her own way back and forth to the bathroom alone. She has diarrhea: she's taken all the Docusate, instead of one or two pills. Worse, she's walking up and down the flight of stairs where she fell before. (I imagine her during that day – one of the last lucid days of her life – watching her own mind fail hour by hour, helpless, abandoned, alone.)

• Lynn, wild-eyed, whispering nonsensical disjointed words and phrases about her hallucinations. We talk about "the guys outside the window" or the "little people in the knitting basket". I reassure her that the shape of this yarn ball was real, but its face and arms were not; that the noise of the dishwasher was real, but it wasn't caused by people in the kitchen. (Very soon, she can no longer talk lucidly and I can no longer understand her. I can no longer be her anchor! To me, that was most isolating and frightening boundary we had to cross.)

Between

Between the living and the dead.

Between losing and finding,
    Forgetting and remembering,
        Releasing and receiving.

Losing my grip on the one now gone.
    Forgetting her skin, forgetting her voice, forgetting her smile.
        Releasing what I cannot hold.
Losing my job as caregiver.
    Forgetting who I was when I existed only for her.
        Releasing what will no longer serve me, can no longer serve her.
Losing death's intimacy.
    Forgetting (-so slowly it fades-) exactly how she left,
        how I half expected to leave with her.
        Releasing the relief in death and the fear in staying alive.

Between the living and the dead.

Finding that love does not leave with the beloved.
    Remembering that every gift is in the moment it is given or received.
        Receiving comfort and love as it is ever offered.
Finding new passions.
    Remembering my old skills and learning new ones.
        Receiving care from others, and caring for myself.
Finding that life has more to offer than death.
    Remembering other new beginnings.
        Receiving the invitation to fear and yet keep breathing.

Losing but not yet lost. Finding but not yet found.
Between the living and the dead.

Grace

Here is my regret and guilt:
rough hooks and ragged rope pulling down the corners of my mouth;
burning plastic wrapped around my neck;
broken bones in my legs;
sharp steel lights stabbing at my eyes;
sirens stuck inside my ears.

Here is what would give it ease:
sobbing until I am done;
telling the story again and again;
curling up until I am healed;
closing my eyes until I see from the inside;
soft words spoken over and over until I fall asleep.

Gently, I lay these days aside. I pour my memories, spill them, empty them out – those that I can; the rest I clutch inside, cherishing even the terror.

Gently, I call myself back. Did I do well? Yes. Did things go wrong? Yes. Is it all exactly as it should be?

Gently, I search for grace. I stare at the ghost of Lynn, at my friends and family, at nurses, doctors, caregivers.

Sometimes I find grace. In perfect timing or unearned knowledge. In curiosity. In utter silence, stillness. Yes and in panic, despair, dread, pounding guilt.

Grace, a warm shoulder during a tough song.

Grace, eyes looking back that are wet like mine.

Grace, a hand on my chest, stronger than my pain.

Grace, a hug from behind, right when my coffee starts collecting tears.

Grace, food appearing when needed, without request or even desire.

Grace, the whisper of my own voice, years from now, reminding me to live.

Licked Clean

Endless weekends of garage sales...

Finally, the last sale, advertised as "Everything free! Saturday only, 10:00 sharp, two garages, no previews, all as-is!"

While eating breakfast cereal, I glance out the window: Holy shit, that's a lot of people!! Milling about, peering around corners, staying carefully off the property line. Eager. Way eager. Scary eager.

10:00 sharp, I go into the front garage, press the button, watch under the slowly rising garage door: Legs! Thousands of purposefully striding, over-eager legs! (Get out of the way!)

"Are you sure this little refrigerator works real good?"
"Everything's as-is."
(Unspoken: "Look, after 20 garage sales it's still here and now it's free, what the hell do you....")

"Hey, somebody's taking all my stuff I've been piling up over there!"
"Sorry."
(–not really.)

"Hi, thanks, this is great! – I know you said only what's not screwed down, but that pegboard is only attached in a couple places...?"
"Let's find a screwdriver."

Within an hour, they've removed the entire contents of two garages half-full of mostly Lynn's stuff. They've licked the place clean.

Licked clean, as in done and over?

No, licked clean as in, I hope it'll help this infected wound start healing.

Home, No More

Vacation over. (Magical!)
Pack up, say goodbyes, exchange addresses, catch the ferry home.
Beautiful drive, clear sky, soft water. Grateful and happy.

Then, creeping fear, anxiety, dread:
What will meet me at the door?
Pain, illness, need? Pills, appointments, scans? Uncertain diagnosis and treatment?

No, now I remember: thank God, that's all over! Relax, it's Ok. I don't have to worry. Endless responsibility and helplessness aren't waiting for me at the door.

No, what's waiting there now is much different:
Nothing.

A New Life

My life, like a broken and dirty window, shows me what I do not want to see:

The pain and loss covering my surface
 demands my attention but reveals nothing.

Sometimes I am able to peer deeper,
 into glaring and distorted reflections of what is behind me,
  horrible, unbelievable but undeniable.

But sometimes, when the light is perfect,
 I can see completely through my life,
  as if into
   someone else's.

Letter to Steve

May 21, 2007
Hello, Steve!

Thank you for you recent, kind letters! I'm sorry my reply here is so much delayed; the reason will become obvious.

I want to talk with you about time. My watch stopped. Why is this important? Because when it happened, time itself stopped. Stopped and then started running backwards; but at the same time, a second timeline also began (different from my old sort of time), and that one runs forward. So now I'm living life in two directions at the same time (backward and forward), and all without even knowing what time ("watch" time) it really is.

This all began when Lynn died. That itself was not a surprise: it's what we were anticipating for nearly ten years. Finally, the doctor gave her the dreaded news that he had no more treatment options to offer, and within two weeks she was dead. (The last week still gives me nightmares, but that's a different story.) Her actual death was probably as good as could be achieved. She was at home with me, surrounded by loving friends and family, competent caring professionals, and her cat. She did not appear to have much pain or fear; and she was at least somewhat aware of her surroundings right until her last breaths.

There were hints about the time thing. The last weekend before her death – when she was still walking a little, and talking, and able to differentiate between hallucination and reality – time stood still. We were together constantly, but not sharing any of the activities we normally did on a weekend. There were no reference points, schedules, regular events, or even needs. Rather, we simply existed, together. Waiting, I suppose; but there was no sense of progress toward something. The waiting itself was timeless. More of a watching than a waiting. There was no now and then, or us and them, or even her and me. If she was dying, then, by god, I was too, and so was the whole world. Or if I was living, then so was she, and us all.

More hints: the last two friends to visit her, just hours before her death, were friends who had known Lynn way before I did; and they told stories about a Lynn from long ago, about someone I never knew.

The last 20 minutes were outrageously hectic. People were coming and going: our friend Cheral and Lynn's sister Lori both arrived back from running errands; Lori's husband arrived from central Washington. The nurse arrived for an unrelated visit. One hospice worker arrived right then to try to give Lynn a bath! Phones were ringing, people were trying to find things and figure out what was going on and do their best to help. And we were all trying to talk to Lynn and tell her what to do next.

The moment of her last exhale, we rang a bell, and everything stopped.

No one knew what to do next. Her sister's husband looked especially lost, being new in town, so I brought over my little computer and showed him the photo album I'd put together of Lynn's old pictures. That was the start of the backwards time. The slide show started with recent pictures: our bald Lynn playing with the cat, watching videos, talking with Cheral. Then the pictures went farther back, to Lynn's vacation trips, with and without me. Farther back, to some photos Lynn had taken before I knew her; farther still, to her family when she was growing up.

Then I went up to the bedroom and fetched Lynn's most precious red velvet pouch. Together we all opened it and talked about the objects inside – where and who they had come from, what they may have meant to Lynn. Again, time reversed and expanded, as we invoked names and events long gone and talked about generations of ancestors.

All this time, I was obsessively replaying events in my head, backwards, starting with the last few minutes, then hours, then days and weeks, then years. And the backwards was also outwards, from the ever narrowing tunnel she and I had been living in the last week, ending with the singularity of her now chilling stillness – outwards to the larger life Lynn had lived in relative health, and expanding further to the vital power she'd wielded years ago. From the constriction of not even being able to get out of bed to pee, outwards, outwards to her knitting dozens of hats for children with cancer, to designing and overseeing the building of her own house, to creating her careers in music and library science. From a life circumscribed by one other person, to a life (rich by comparison) full of doctors and nurses, to a life brimming with good old friends having shared interests I'd never imagined.

More and more the Lynn I knew moved backwards in time, and expanded outwards, when stories were told during her cremation ceremony and reception. As friends materialized from names in an address book. As old pictures appeared and were added to the album. And as my memories of the horrors of the past week were gradually replaced in importance and vividness with earlier, bigger, sweeter memories I'd lost, or never had.

At the same time, my life was also (in a very different way than before) moving forwards. Seeds were planted and started to grow: hints of fresh and changing relationships, dreams of travel, whispers of openings and movements. Subtle new desires, new directions. Tender emotions and meanings, both painful and blissful. This was not ordinary time; it was time as experienced in an ecstatic state, and I had to speak carefully to ordinary people, those who couldn't see the translucent morphing landscape in which I was now moving.

And my watch stopped. There wasn't time, of course, to get a new watch battery. Besides, time didn't matter: sisters (hers, and mine) were there to do scheduling, plan things, get me where I needed to be on time. No, the only time I needed to attend now was on the inside, and I could afford to let the outside warp to accommodate it.

After the sisters left and the tasks pretty much ended, the house itself fell with me into a quiet timelessness. All the old time markings – pills to be given on time, TV or radio programs turned on or recorded on time, doctor appointments reached on time, toiletries accomplished on time, meals prepared on time – simply disappeared. When an object appeared in front of me, it held my attention until it didn't. If I picked up a magazine, I could read it until I was done. If I began writing a letter, I could write until I finished, or tired of it. If I dozed off, I could sleep until I awoke.

If I played with the cat, I could continue until one of us desired to do something else. And then whatever else I did, I did until I wanted the next thing. Sometimes the next thing didn't appear right away; then there was a pause with nothing happening, and then after a while, the next thing would happen.

It's a very odd kind of time that allows things to start and stop by themselves.

Only the cat remained pegged to the clock: 9:30, breakfast-time. 5:30, suppertime. 10:30, nighttime munchies. Or else: bedlam!

Eventually, slowly, the world impinges. More events each day happen according to outside time. The ecstatic state fades. The gigantic archetypical Lynn achieves mythic proportions and turns to stone, unchanging now forever more – just losing color and gathering dust. My eating times and the cat's, like menses in a household, become locked to the same schedule. Time resumes its normal gait and grip.

Almost. I'm still not wearing my watch, though. It's stopped.

I'll write more. I hope you're well – stay in touch!

-John

Benedictions

Lynn –

You are, in ways death cannot change, part of my soul.

You gave me your trust, as you could give it to no one else. You shared your infirmities, your losses, your diminishment. Without apology or self deprecation or comparison, you gave me the right to see you as no one else was allowed to. You gave me your presence in the last days and hours and minutes of your life. You gave me the last of your physical self, and you showed me your precious death.

I respond to that trust by claiming, now, finally, that it is deserved. I am, always, to the best of my ability, a trustworthy and faithful man.

EPILOG – 2010

Another House

My mind flies to another woods.
    To a house barely visible, barely reachable.
    A clearing barely noticeable.
    A person not much different from the local fauna.

My mind flies to barely a promise, a risk, a chance in a lifetime, against all odds.
An understanding between two people, an agreement invented naked in a meadow out of thin air, disobeying all rules of logic, practically impossible.
A delicate ancient new friendship, recreated now, and now, and now, and long ago.

My mind touches, barely, briefly, a possible answer to many questions, a gift from many challenges, a resolution of much heartache.
    A verdant glen born from forest fire.
    A solace to aching travelers.
    A healing fragrance.

My mind, like an eagle, circles on the warm wind above the woods, above the promise – watching, waiting, barely moving.

Meanwhile, in that other woods, in that house barely visible, the dove of my heart has nested in her eaves.

POSTSCRIPT – 2019

Dreams

During the first few years after her death, Lynn visited me several times in dreams. The first time I heard from her, she was very excited to tell me that she was teaching a class. She described it as "a dream class for young women"; I understood that to mean she was talking to girls in their dreams, teaching and counseling to help them understand their lives better and make wise choices. This was exactly the kind of thing she loved doing when alive! In my dream Lynn was exhilarated and joyous, literally glowing, wearing an elegant white flowing gown. I think she was an angel.

The last time I heard from her she seemed small; again she appeared in a white gown, but this one was more like an old fashioned baptismal dress, much longer than she was. She only said, in a small voice, that she couldn't talk now. I understood that she was reincarnating, and she was perhaps already a baby, too young to speak.

I have also had many realistic dreams about Lynn in which I'm surprised or shocked to see her still alive in the present moment: I know for sure she's dead, but here she is, acting otherwise. I think about asking her if she shouldn't be dead now, but I never do. After several of these dreams, I started realizing inside the dream that I must be dreaming: if Lynn's still alive, it's a dream. I could then continue the dream without having to wonder what she's doing back here again and how she did it. (I understand that though these were about her and seemed completely life-like, Lynn herself was never present with me in this type of dream: they had a very different feeling from the ones in which she actually came in spirit to visit me.)

The End

I don't eat granola in the middle of the night anymore.

Kismitt still purrs, squirms, licks my hand, when she comes up to visit me in the morning just before it's time to get up. Now she needs stair steps to get onto the bed, though. She's getting older. It's often hard for her to walk; I can tell when her hips hurt. She sleeps more. She goes outside less often, and then stays closer to the door. I think her world is getting smaller.

And *I'm* getting older.

My life is fine. It's excellent. I'm happy, most of the time, busy doing things I enjoy. My beloved and I share our lives together like a pea in a pod. I am always surrounded by loving friends, some I've known for decades, some I meet as I go. And some I see less often, and they slip away. So I spend more time with myself, and I'm content with that. I'm content. Everything turned out Ok.

But I'm slowing down. I don't walk as far or as fast, and one knee or the other sometimes hurts. I sleep more. I'm not as strong, and I make more mistakes. Names are hard for me to remember; I forget common words sometimes. My abilities are changing. Maybe my world is getting smaller – or maybe not.

Since Lynn left, I've seen some other people die, and some almost die, and some wish they could die. I've experienced what it's like to die myself, and I've seen what happens next. I've spent a little time in heaven. (I looked for Lynn there, but as she hinted in the dream, she was apparently busy elsewhere. I did see my mother, though.) I understand that the line defined by dying is less sharp than I had thought, and less important. I feel my self stretching across that line.

Sometimes I bow in respect to an old man – a future self, or a past self – who cannot walk or cannot talk or cannot see. Sometimes I bow in respect to a vibrant young woman, to a dark skinned child, to a quiet monk. I am all of those. I am learning, as I meet my selves, that I'm larger than I ever imagined. Death is necessary, for that enlargement, and death also does the teaching.

So it calls to me. There's no hurry, it's not going anywhere; and I'm still busy here doing things that I love.

But slowly, very slowly — finally — I'm following Lynn.

Gratitude

To Cheral, my personal assistant at the time, for her kind and loving care for both Lynn and me. (The title "The Friday Lynn" is from Cheral.)

To Lynn's sister Lori for her love expressed in management of Lynn's physical affairs: she worried so we needn't. (I think she never got any scarves.)

To my big sister Caryl, my favorite teacher of life and love ever since childhood, who shared her own honest grief and then came to share mine. ("How to talk to people who are alive" started with ideas from Caryl.)

To my family and friends; to Kathy and her friends; to Lynn's friends, support groups and work mates: every day of our journey, theirs were the shoulders we knew we could lean on.

To Vicky Edmonds for leading the poetry workshop (the vacation in "Home No More") where some of these poems were born.

To Bobbie, friend and fellow tenor, for her help with the manuscript.

To Eva-Maria for always expanding my ideas of what's possible.

To my ministers Colette Mercier and Eric O'del, to my sangha, and to my entire spiritual community for encouragement, inspiration and holy witness.

To the deeply caring doctors, nurses and staff of Swedish Cancer Institute; especially to Sylvia Farias and the Caregivers Support Group, where the unthinkable could be spoken.

To Ginny and her family for opening their souls to Ghania and me.

To my partner Ghania jami, demolisher and embracer, soulmate, playmate and guide, for welcoming me back to life.

And, of course, to Kismitt, for being the cat.

For purchase information or for online versions of this book,
as well as other poetry and essays by the author,
please "Follow" me at
https://patiofarms.blogspot.com/
and navigate to the "Dark Discourse with the Sleepy Cat" page.

Dark Discourse with the Sleepy Cat
Copyright © John Nelson 2019
All Rights Reserved

Cover design, book design and all images by John Nelson
v2.3

Built with Baskerville in Pages mainly on Ginny's old MacBook Air
in an Amtrak club car and a Seattle houseboat,
with Kismitt on my lap.

Patio Farms Press

www.ingramcontent.com/pod-product-compliance
Lightning Source LLC
Chambersburg PA
CBHW071409290426
44108CB00014B/1751